Old Havana, Cuba, the City of Columns

A TRAVEL PHOTO ART BOOK

LAINE CUNNINGHAM

Old Havana, Cuba, the City of Columns

A Travel Photo Art Book

Published by Sun Dogs Creations
Changing the World One Book at a Time
Print ISBN: 978-1-951389-23-9

Cover Image by Laine Cunningham
Cover Design by Angel Leya

Copyright © 2024 Laine Cunningham

All rights reserved. No part of this book may be reproduced in any form or by any means, electronic, mechanical, digital, photocopying or recording, except for the inclusion in a review, without permission in writing from the publisher.

The UNESCO World Heritage site known as Old Havana has maintained an extraordinary degree of its original character. Its narrow streets range through a host of historic sites from Castillo del Morro to the National Capitol. A number of gorgeous plazas offer plenty of coffee shops and restaurants.

While the well-known sites attract lots of visitors, the streets themselves are a true joy to stroll along. Tiny parks sparkle with sunlight and stay cool with shade trees. Breezes bring cooler air off the harbor near the port, and the sounds of Cuban music add a lively element to the backdrop of vibrant buildings.

From dawn through the night, Old Havana is possibly the most unique city in the world.

HUB

BUBBLES

CRIMP

BARRANCA

CARNIVAL

AXIAL

INLAY

MULTIPLES

MERCY

FIZZ

MOONTIDE

APPLIQUE

GRIP

RUNDLE

CIRRUS

EQUILIBRIUM

LIONS

FULFILLED

HEADDRESS

GAMBOL

LEISURE

LIMPET

PRESENCE

DAPPER

CONFERENCE

AWAIT

BOLTED

INSIGNIA

MOUSE

LONER

JABBER

LOOK

GREYHOUND

ARTICULATE

GALLERY

SWASH

TWISTER

THRESH

PEEPS

MIDWAY

WAYFARER

HALCYON

VIRTU

WINDSWEPT

TITLES IN THIS SERIES

Havana, Cuba
Old Havana, Cuba, the City of Columns
The Malecón, Havana, Cuba
Central Havana, Cuba
Vedado, Havana's Forbidden Neighborhood
Regla, the Quieter Side of Havana, Cuba
Miramar, Havana, Cuba
Streets of Havana, Cuba
Classic Cars of Cuba
Classic Cars of Old Havana, Cuba
Classic Cars of Havana, Cuba
Spanish Colonial Havana, Cuba
Gardens of Havana, Cuba
Verge Gardens of Havana, Cuba
Cats of Havana, Cuba
Colón Cemetery, Cuba
National Art Schools of Havana, Cuba

www.ingramcontent.com/pod-product-compliance
Lightning Source LLC
Chambersburg PA
CBHW040002080526
44586CB00027B/2849